D1540374

OPEN COURT READING

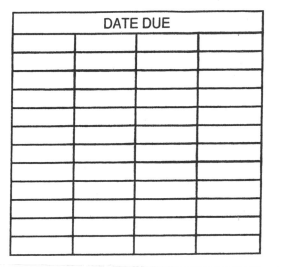

DATE DUE

CMC.4200.S774o.Gr.1.2002.P6
Reteach: Comprehension and Lang
uage Arts Skills

Jennie Huizenga Memorial Library
TRINITY CHRISTIAN COLLEGE
6601 W. COLLEGE DRIVE
PALOS HEIGHTS, IL 60463

GAYLORD M2G

A Division of The McGraw·Hill Companies

Columbus, Ohio

www.sra4kids.com

SRA/McGraw-Hill

A Division of The McGraw·Hill Companies

Copyright © 2002 by SRA/McGraw-Hill.

All rights reserved. Except as permitted under the United States Copyright Act, no part of this publication may be reproduced or distributed in any form or by any means, or stored in a database or retrieval system, without the prior written permission of the publisher, unless otherwise indicated.

Send all inquiries to:
SRA/McGraw-Hill
8787 Orion Place
Columbus, OH 43240-4027

Printed in the United States of America.

ISBN 0-07-572027-2

2 3 4 5 6 7 8 9 POH 07 06 05 04 03 02

Table of Contents

▶Capital Letters

Directions: Read the words next to each picture. Circle the word that begins with a capital letter.

MECHANICS

> **Rule** The names of people and pets begin with a capital letter.
> **Example** Maria   Tony   Spot

Practice

   (Nate)   nate

   gwen   (Gwen)

   (Socks)   socks

   pedro   (Pedro)

UNIT 1   Let's Read! • **Lesson 2** *The Purple Cow*

▶ Writing Words

Directions: Write the letters that finish each word.

Rule Letters make words.
Example

_____ rat   _____ duck

 Practice

| top | jam | pig | hen |

1. p_____ **ig**   2. j_____ **am**

3. h_____ **en**   4. t_____ **op**

WRITER'S CRAFT

▶ Capital Letters: Cities and States

MECHANICS

> **Rule** Names of cities and states begin with a capital letter.
> **Example** Freeport, Maine
> Houston, Texas

Practice

1. iowa ___**Iowa**___

2. florida ___**Florida**___

3. denver ___**Denver**___

4. oregon ___**Oregon**___

▶Order Words

Rule Some words tell the order things happen.
Example first   next   last

Directions: Label the pictures 1,2,3 to show when they happen.

Practice

_____
- - - - - - - - - - - - - - - - - -
2
_____

_____
- - - - - - - - - - - - - - - - - -
3
_____

_____
- - - - - - - - - - - - - - - - - -
1
_____

WRITER'S CRAFT

▶ Sentences

MECHANICS

> **Rule** Sentences start with capital letters. Sentences that tell something end with periods.
> **Example** It is harvest time.

Directions: Read each sentence. Circle the word that should begin with a capital letter. Write the capital letter on the line. Put a period at the end of each sentence.

Practice

1. _____ **J** _____ (johnny) likes apples __._

2. _____ **A** _____ (apples) grow on trees __._

3. _____ **H** _____ (he) picks apples in the fall __._

4. _____ **T** _____ (the) basket is full __._

Sentences • Reteach: Comprehension and Language Arts Skills

▶ Writing Sentences

Directions: Look at the picture. Write sentences using the words. Use a capital letter and end mark.

> **Rule** Sentences begin with a capital letter. Many sentences end with periods.
> **Example** Frogs jump.

Practice

1. Bats   fly.

_____

Bats fly.

_____

2. Fish   swim.

- - - - - - - - - - - - - - - - - - -

Fish swim.

_____

3. The dog   jumps.

_____

- - - - - - - - - - - - - - - - - - -

The dog jumps.

_____

4. Kittens   play.

- - - - - - - - - - - - - - - - - - -

Kittens play.

_____

WRITER'S CRAFT

▶Comparing and Contrasting

Directions: Circle A if the pictures are alike and D if the pictures are different. The first one is done for you.

1.

A (D)

2. 

(A) D

3.

(A) D

4.

A (D)

Comparing and Contrasting • Reteach: Comprehension
and Language Arts Skills

▶**Comparing and Contrasting**

Directions: Write *A* if the picture shows things that are alike and *D* if the picture shows things that are different.

5.

_____

_ _ _ _ _ _ _ _ _ _ _ _ _ _ _ _ _ _ _

A

6.

_____

_ _ _ _ _ _ _ _ _ _ _ _ _ _ _ _ _ _ _

A

7.

_____

_ _ _ _ _ _ _ _ _ _ _ _ _ _ _ _ _ _ _

D

8.

_____

_ _ _ _ _ _ _ _ _ _ _ _ _ _ _ _ _ _ _

D

COMPREHENSION

▶ Adjectives

> **Rule** Describing words tell more about something.
> **Example** It is a *sunny* day.

Practice

Directions: Write the word that describes each picture.

small	hot	pretty	tall

small

pretty

hot

tall

Adjectives • Reteach: Comprehension
and Language Arts Skills

GRAMMAR/USAGE

UNIT 2 Animals • **Lesson 2** *Raccoons*

▶Using Adjectives

Rule Adjectives describe naming words.
Example furry rabbit

Practice

| small | spotted | muddy | sleepy |

1. muddy

2. small

3. sleepy

4. spotted

WRITER'S CRAFT

Reteach: Comprehension • *Using Adjectives*
and Language Arts Skills

UNIT 2 • Lesson 2 **11**

▶Types of Sentences

GRAMMAR USAGE

Directions: Listen to each sentence. Circle each sentence that is a question and underline each sentence that shows strong feeling.

Rule	**Example**
▸Some sentences tell.	▸I am six years old.
▸Some sentences ask.	▸How old are you?
▸Some sentences show strong feeling.	▸I am six years old, too!

Practice

1. What a hot day!

2. Can you skip?

3. That is a big bug!

4. We can sit on the grass.

5. Do you like to swing?

▶ Main Idea and Details

Main idea: Dressing for a winter day
Details:

Directions: Read the main idea to the students. Have them circle the picture that does not belong.

COMPREHENSION

▶ Main Idea and Details

Main idea: Painting a house

Details:

Directions: Read the main idea to the students. Have them draw an X on the picture that does not belong.

COMPREHENSION

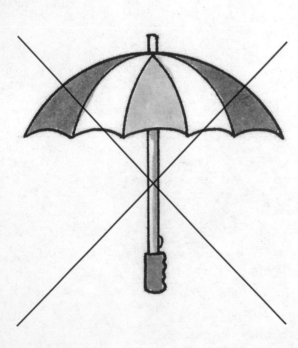

Main Idea and Details • Reteach: Comprehension
and Language Arts Skills

▶ Writing Sentences

Directions: Look at the picture. Read the sentence. Write a period, question mark, or exclamation point at the end of each sentence.

Rule	**Example**
▶ Some sentences tell. They end with a **.**	▶ Raccoons catch their food.
▶ Some sentences ask. They end with a **?**	▶ What do raccoons eat?
▶ Some sentences show strong feeling. They end with a **!**	▶ Raccoons eat lots of fish!

Practice

1. Do kangaroos run _____**?**_____

2. Kangaroos hop _____**.**_____

3. Kangaroos hop very fast _____**!**_____

4. Kangaroos have strong legs ___**.** or **!**___

Directions: Circle the adjective that describes the underlined word in each sentence. Put the correct end mark at the end of each sentence.

▶Review

GRAMMAR USAGE

> **Rule** Describing words tell more about something.
> **Example** We can play on the **green** grass.

> **Rule**
> ▶ Sentences that tell end with a **period**.
> ▶ Sentences that ask end with a **question mark**.
> ▶ Sentences that show strong feeling end with an **exclamation point**.

Practice

1. I have a (new) <u>mitt</u> _____ .

2. Who can swing the (yellow) <u>bat</u> _____ ?

3. Hurray, what a (fun) <u>game</u> _____ !

Review • Reteach: Comprehension and Language Arts Skills

UNIT 2 Animals • **Lesson 12** *The Hermit Crab*

▶ Writing Descriptions

> **Rule** Writers describe things.
> **Example** Snails move **slowly**. They have **soft** bodies and **hard** shells.

Practice

Directions: Look at the picture. Read the sentence. Write the words from the box to complete the description.

WRITER'S CRAFT

| slowly | two big | four strong | long |

1. An elephant has _____ **two big** _____ ears.

2. An elephant has a _____ **long** _____ trunk.

3. An elephant walks with _____ **four strong** _____ legs.

4. An elephant walks _____ **slowly** _____ .

▶ # Drawing Conclusions

Directions: Read each sentence and circle the word or words that best describe the picture.

1. Pam is (sad) not sad).

2. Dan is (mad, not mad).

Drawing Conclusions • Reteach: Comprehension
and Language Arts Skills

UNIT 2 Animals • **Lesson 14** *The Hermit Crab*

▶ Drawing Conclusions

Directions: Look at the picture. Read each sentence to the students. Have them circle Yes or No to tell whether the sentence describes the picture.

COMPREHENSION

1. The children are on a playground.   Yes   (No)

2. The children are listening.   (Yes)   No

3. They like the story.   (Yes)   No

UNIT 3 THINGS THAT GO • **Lesson I** *Unit Introduction*

▶ Possessive Nouns

Directions: Write the words that tell who or what owns each object.
The first one is done for you.

> **Rule** Add **'s** to a noun to show ownership.
> **Example** Meg's coat
>   bird's nest

Practice

1. The cow has a bell.

cow's bell

2. Ron has a lizard.

Ron's lizard

3. The farmer has a pond.

farmer's pond

4. Jill has a tree.

Jill's tree

Possessive Nouns • Reteach: Comprehension
and Language Arts Skills

GRAMMAR AND USAGE

▶Staying on Topic

Rule Writers write lists of words that belong together.

Practice

Directions: Circle the words that belong in a list.

Baseball

 (ball)

 (bat)

 pin

 (mitt)

WRITER'S CRAFT

▶ # Singular and Plural Nouns

Directions: Circle the word that tells about the picture. Then, draw a picture to match the last word.

GRAMMAR AND USAGE

> **Rule** Add **s** to a noun to show that there is more than one.
>
> **Example** book   books

Practice

1.

   ham   (hams)

2.

   (pan)   pans

3. | drawing of more than one ant |
   | --- |

   ants

▶ Sensory Details

> **Rule** Writers write words to tell how something looks, feels, smells, sounds, and tastes.

Practice

Directions: Look at the picture. Write the word that describes it.

loud	shiny	sweet	bumpy	hot

1. **sweet** jam

2. **bumpy** shell

3. **loud** bell

4. **hot** soup

5. **shiny** ring

WRITER'S CRAFT

►Comparing and Contrasting

Directions: Circle the item in each row that is different.

1.

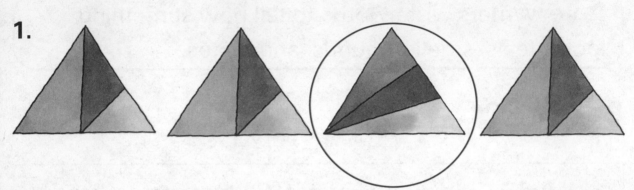

2.

3.

Comparing and Contrasting • Reteach: Comprehension
and Language Arts Skills

▶Comparing and Contrasting

Directions: Circle the word or words that tell how the animals are alike.

COMPREHENSION

1.

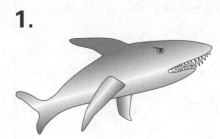  

(**sharp teeth**) live in water

2.

six legs (**fly**)

3.

(**have stripes**) have skinny tails

▶Review

GRAMMAR AND USAGE

Directions: Read each sentence. Write the possessive noun on the line. Then underline the singular nouns and circle the plural nouns.

Rule	**Example**
▶ Add **'s** to a noun or name to show ownership.	▶ Peter's bike
	the bike's wheels
▶ Add **s** to a noun to show that there is more than one.	▶ bike bikes

Practice

1. My mom's (keys) are lost.   **mom's**

2. The car's <u>door</u> is stuck.   **car's**

3. Becky's (cats) are white and orange.   **Becky's**

4. The cat's <u>toy</u> is pink.   **cat's**

Review • Reteach: Comprehension
and Language Arts Skills

▶Order Words

Directions: Look at the pictures. Write the correct order word next to each picture.

> **Rule** Order words tell the order things happen.
>
> first   next   then   last

Practice

first   next   last

1. _____

   next

2. _____

   last

3. _____

   first

WRITER'S CRAFT

▶Capitalization

Directions: Read each sentence. Circle each letter that should be a capital. Then write the capital letter above it. The first one is done for you.

MECHANICS

> **Rule** Days and months begin with a capital letter.
> **Example** Monday   January

Practice

1. Today is the first ⓢaturday in ⓜay.
                      S   M

2. The fruit stand is open in ⓙuly and ⓐugust.
                              J   A

3. Music class is on ⓣuesdays and ⓣhursdays.
                     T   T

4. This year my birthday is on ⓕriday, ⓜarch 6.
                               F   M

▶Classifying and Categorizing

Directions: Draw lines to match the pictures that belong together.

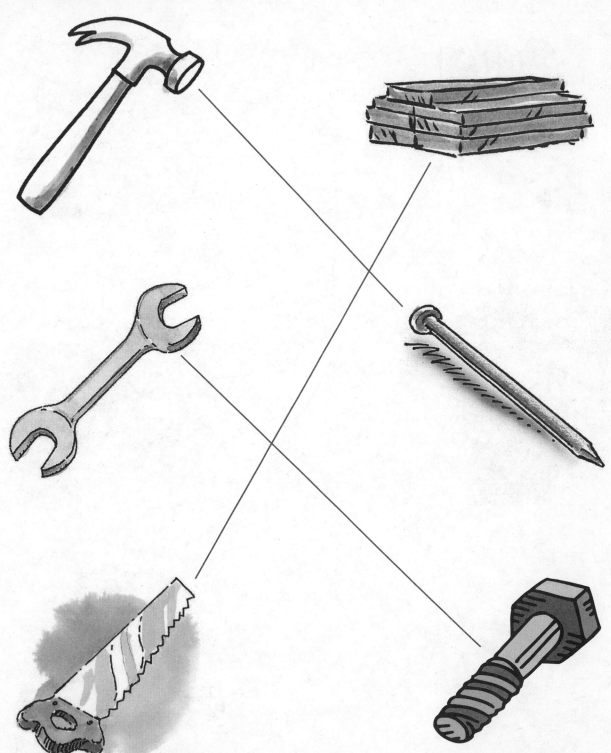

COMPREHENSION

▶Classifying and Categorizing

COMPREHENSION

Classifying and Categorizing • Reteach: Comprehension and Language Arts Skills

▶ Who, What, Where, and When

Directions: Match the word to the picture that answers the question.

> **Rule** Writers tell **who**, **what** happens, **where** something happens and **when** something happens to be sure readers understand.

Practice

1. who

2. what

3. where

4. when

WRITER'S CRAFT

▶ End Punctuation

MECHANICS

> **Rule** Sentences end with ., ?, or !.
> **Example** This is a cake. Do you like cake? I love cake!

Practice

1. Ben opens the paint can _____**.**____

2. Blue paint spills all over the floor ___**! or .**___

3. What a mess _____**!**_____

4. How can we clean it _____**?**_____

5. We can use these rags _____**.**____

End Punctuation • Reteach: Comprehension and Language Arts Skills

▶Personal Letter

> **Rule** A friendly letter has the **date**, a **greeting**, a **message**, a **closing** and **your name**.

Practice

Directions: Write the names of the parts of a letter where they belong.

_____

_____ **Date** _____ May 4, 2003

_____

_____ **Greeting** _____ Dear Jacob,

_____ **message** _____ We went to my aunt's farm. We fed the chickens. We fed the cows. We picked apples. Have you ever been on a farm?

_____ **Closing** _____ Your friend,

_____ **Name** _____ Sue

WRITER'S CRAFT

Name _____ Date _____

▶ Capitalization and End Punctuation

MECHANICS

Rule	**Example**
▸ Days and months begin with capital letters.	▸ Saturday April
▸ Sentences end with ., ?, or !.	▸ The doorbell rang. Who's there? Surprise!

Practice

1. When does Nan feed the ducks _____ **?** _____

2. Nan feeds the ducks in (july) _____ **·** _____

3. She goes to the pond every (tuesday) _____ **·** _____

4. Will the pond be frozen in (february) _____ **?** _____

5. Fly away duck _____ **!** _____

▶ Audience and Purpose

Rule Writers think about who will read their writing. Then they think about what they want to tell them.

Practice

Directions: Draw a line from the audience or purpose to the correct piece of writing.

1. shoppers

2. tell facts about a topic

3. a friend

4. write ideas

WRITER'S CRAFT

▶Longer Sentences

Directions: Read the sentence. Write the correct word to make the sentence longer.

WRITER'S CRAFT

> **Rule** Longer sentences tell readers more. Write words that tell **how**, **when**, and **where**.

Practice

| in the yard | sometimes | loudly |

1. When? _____

Dogs bark ____**sometimes**____ .

2. How? _____

Dogs bark ____**loudly**____ .

3. Where? _____

Dogs bark ____**in the yard**____ .

Longer Sentences • Reteach: Comprehension and Language Arts Skills

▶ Adjectives

Directions: Read each sentence. Write the adjective from the box that correctly completes each sentence.

> **Rule** Adjectives are words used to describe nouns.
> **Example** Brad has a **red** shirt. His shirt is **red**.

Practice

silver	chilly	sharp	soft

1. Dad cut the meat with a _____ sharp _____ knife.

2. The _____ silver _____ plane moved down the runway.

3. Ruth took a walk on a _____ chilly _____ day.

4. The dog slept on a _____ soft _____ pillow.

GRAMMAR AND USAGE

▶ Main Idea and Details

COMPREHENSION

Main idea: Day at School
Details:

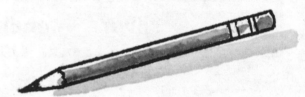

Main idea: Day at the Farm
Details:

Directions: Put an X through the picture that is not a detail that supports the main idea given.

COMPREHENSION

Directions: Write the correct order word in each sentence.

◤ **WRITER'S CRAFT**

► # Order Words

> **Rule** Order words tell the order things happen.
> **Example** first   next   then   last

Practice

First	Next	Then	Last

1. _____Last_____, we mailed it at the post office.

2. _____Then_____, we wrapped it.

3. _____First_____, Mom got a gift at the store.

4. _____Next_____, we put it in a box.

40 UNIT 5 • Lesson 3

Order Words • Reteach: Comprehension
and Language Arts Skills

▶Verbs

Directions: Read each sentence. Circle the word that shows action in each sentence.

> **Rule** Verbs show action.
> **Example** The children **play** at the park.

Practice

1. Pete and Bill (skate) to the park.

2. Jane (meets) them at the park.

3. Bill (sits) on a bench.

4. Jane and Pete (race) up a ramp.

5. Bill (cheers) for them.

GRAMMAR AND USAGE

▶Review

GRAMMAR USAGE

Directions: Read each sentence. Draw a line under the word or words that describe a noun. Circle the noun that they describe. Put a box around the verb in each sentence. The first one is done for you.

Rule	**Example**
▶Adjectives are words used to describe nouns.	▶A **scaly** lizard crawls in the sand.
▶Verbs show action.	▶A scaly lizard **crawls** in the sand.

Practice

1. <u>Ten</u> (fish) [swim] upstream.

2. A <u>black</u> (crow) [sits] on a fence.

3. The bear [eats] <u>sweet</u> <u>sticky</u> (honey.)

4. The <u>gray</u> (wolves) [howl] at the moon.

5. A <u>tiny</u> <u>white</u> (mouse) [runs] in the field.

6. The owl's <u>sharp</u> (eyes) [see] the mouse.

Review • Reteach: Comprehension and Language Arts Skills

▶Commas in a Series

> **Rule** Commas are used in lists of three or more.
> **Example** I like apples, bananas, and pears.

Practice

Directions: Read each sentence. Write the commas where they belong.

1. Tammy,Joel,Molly,and Andrew went for a picnic.

2. Molly brought plates,cups,and napkins.

3. Joel carried the picnic basket,drinks,and blanket.

4. The children ate bread,cheese,and bananas.

MECHANICS

►Classifying and Categorizing

Directions: Find the word in the box that belongs with each picture. Then write the word on the line below.

COMPREHENSION

pig	clam	fish
eel	moose	ant

water

fish

land

moose

eel

pig

clam

ant

► Classifying and Categorizing

COMPREHENSION

Directions: Find the word in the box that belongs with each word and picture and write the word on the line. The first one is done for you.

pencil	jam	thread	fries

1. needle and thread

2. burger and fries

3. toast and jam

4. paper and pencil

▶ A Paragraph that Explains

WRITER'S CRAFT

> **Rule** Some paragraphs explain how to do something. The first sentence tells what they are going to explain. The other sentences tell each step in order.

Practice

First, they dig open the ant nest.

Last, they lick up the ants.

Anteaters eat ants.

Next, they stick out their long tongues.

_____

_____

Anteaters eat ants. First, they dig open the ant nest.

_____

_____

Next, they stick out their long tongues. Last, they lick up

_____

_____

the ants.

_____

_____

_____

▶Capitalization: Cities and States

Directions: Read each sentence. Underline the word or words that should begin with a capital letter. Write the capital letter above the words.

> **Rule** The names of cities and states always begin with a capital letter.
> **Example** Detroit, Michigan

Practice

1. My family is from california.
   C

2. Aunt Poly lives in santa monica.
   S   M

3. Uncle Rick works in los angeles.
   L   A

4. We can drive to Grandma's house in pasadena.
   P

5. We took an airplane to denver, colorado.
   D   C

6. Someday I'd like to visit orlando, florida.
   O   F

MECHANICS

UNIT 6 Journeys • **Lesson 8** *Me on the Map*

WRITER'S CRAFT

▶ Place and Location Words

> ▶ Writers write words to tell where people, places, and things are.

Directions: Look at each picture. Write the word that tells where.

Practice

over	behind	under	between

1. The mice walk  the jars.

2. Dad lays a blanket over the baby.

3. The chipmunk is  the basket.

4. The ladybug is  the plant.

Place and Location Words • Reteach: Comprehension and Language Arts Skills

▶Making Inferences

Directions: Look at the picture. Based on the clues in the picture, circle the sentences that best describe what's happening.

(The dog wants to go outside.)

The dog wants to take a nap.

(The dog wants to chase the squirrel and birds.)

The birds and squirrel see the dog.

COMPREHENSION

▶ Making Inferences

COMPREHENSION

Directions: Look at the picture. Based on the clues in the picture, mark an X next to the sentences that best describe what is happening.

_____ The duck doesn't see the girl.

_**X**_ The duck is hungry.

_**X**_ The girl wants to feed the duck.

_____ The girl likes dogs.

Making Inferences • Reteach: Comprehension
and Language Arts Skills

UNIT 6 Journeys • **Lesson II** *The Special Day*

►Review

> **Rule** Commas are used in lists of three or more.
> **Example** I collect stickers, stamps, and marbles.

> **Rule** Cities and states begin with a capital letter.
> **Example** **P**hiladelphia, **P**ennsylvania

Practice

1. kansas city, st. louis, and springfield are cities in missouri.

2. The Delmarva Peninsula is part of delaware, maryland, and virginia.

3. The White House, the Lincoln Memorial, and the Smithsonian are in washington D.C..

4. wisconsin, michigan, indiana, and illinois all border Lake Michigan.

5. arizona, colorado, new mexico, and utah meet at four corners.

6. nashville, raleigh, and columbia are capital cities.

MECHANICS

Reteach: Comprehension • *Review* and Language Arts Skills

► Form of a Paragraph

Directions: Read the paragraph. Circle the sentence that should be first.

WRITER'S CRAFT

> **Rule** Writers use sentences that go together to write a paragraph. The first sentence tells what the paragraph is about.
>
> **Example** Trucks take many things to places. They take food to markets. They take mail to post offices. They take cans to a recycle center. Trucks move a lot!

Practice

They use them to plow land. Then they use them to help plant seeds. (Farmers use tractors.) Farmers even use tractors to help them pick the crops.

Form of a Paragraph • Reteach: Comprehension and Language Arts Skills

Past Tense Verbs

Rule Add **–ed** to a verb to show that it already happened.
Example I **called** Grandma last week.

Rule Some verbs change to show that something already happened. They don't use **–ed**.
Example I run fast. Yesterday I **ran** fast.

Practice Read the sentence. Circle the word that tells what already happened.

1. My family (moved) to a new house.

2. We (packed) our things.

3. I (said) goodbye to my old friends.

4. Then I (made) a new friend!

GRAMMAR AND USAGE

▶ Concept Words

VOCABULARY

> **Rule** A **concept word** is the name of an idea. Look for words that tell about an unfamiliar concept to find its meaning.

Practice Circle the words that describe each concept word.

Love

hat (kindness) box yard (respect) (caring)

Music

(song) (drum) truck store (dance) tree

Concept Words • Reteach: Comprehension and Language Arts Skills

▶ Sound Spelling Review

Rule	**Example**
▶Long-vowel sounds can be spelled with different patterns.	▶toad so tote

Practice Circle the word that completes each sentence. Write the word on the line.

_____

1. I _____**wrote**_____ my name with a pencil.

   (wrote)   go

_____

2. Let's _____**go**_____ to the store.

   wrote   (go)

_____

3. My brother is _____**three**_____ years old.

   (three)   free

_____

4. I set the butterfly _____**free**_____.

   three   (free)

SPELLING

▶ Exact Words

> **Rule** Writers use exact naming words, words that describe, and action words.

Practice Read each sentence. Circle the exact word. Write the word in the sentence.

1. Look at the _____colorful_____ butterfly.

   pretty   (colorful)

2. It _____flutters_____ its wings.

   moves   (flutters)

3. Butterflies _____sip_____ nectar from flowers.

   eat   (sip)

4. Butterflies _____curl_____ up their tongues after eating.

   (curl)   bring

Exact Words • Reteach: Comprehension and Language Arts Skills

WRITER'S CRAFT

►Cause and Effect

►**Read each sentence that tells what happened. Then circle the sentence that tells why.**

1. Tad ran down the street after his dog.

   a. His dog ate some dog food.

   (b. His dog broke the leash.)

2. The smoke alarm went off.

   (a. The frying pan was on fire.)

   b. The bathtub was filled with water.

3. Shane scratched his legs and arms.

   a. Shane stayed up late to read his book.

   (b. Shane got bug bites when he walked in the woods.)

4. There were big puddles in the street.

   a. The sun was shining.

   (b. It had rained all night.)

5. The flowers were dead.

   (a. The flowers were not watered.)

   b. The flowers were planted in May.

COMPREHENSION

▶ Cause and Effect

▶Draw a line to the sentence that tells what happened next.

1. Mason ate too much at the fair.

The bird flew away.

2. A cat climbed the tree.

Jane opened her umbrella.

3. Dad's pen broke open.

The flowers on the trees are blooming.

4. It is springtime.

He felt sick.

5. It started to rain.

He got ink all over his hands.

COMPREHENSION

Cause and Effect • Reteach: Comprehension and Language Arts Skills

▶Antonyms

Rule Antonyms are opposites.

Example up   down

Practice Draw a line from each word to its antonym.

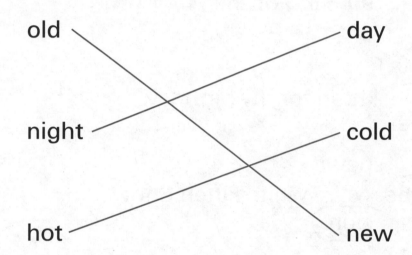

old   day

night   cold

hot   new

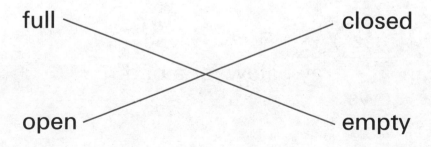

full   closed

open   empty

VOCABULARY

Sound Spelling Review

SPELLING

> **Rule** The /ū/ sound can be spelled:
> **Example** u_e   cube
>   ew   chew
>   _ue   blue

Practice Read the sentences. Circle the correct spelling of the /ū/ word.

(cute)

1. I got a   kitten for my birthday.
       cuet

              pewr
2. I named the   white kitten Snow.
          (pure)

    fue
3. A   of my friends came over to play with Snow.
(few)

        (use)
4. Snow can   my pillow for a bed.
      ews

▶ Pronouns

> **Rule** A pronoun takes the place of a noun.
> **Example** Dan catches the ball. **He** catches **it**.

Practice Look at each picture. Read the sentence. Write the correct pronoun on the line.

they	it	you	he

1. _____**He**_____ can catch.

2. _____**They**_____ ride the bus.

3. _____**You**_____ may have a cookie.

4. _____**It**_____ talks a lot.

GRAMMAR AND USAGE

UNIT 7 Keep Trying • **Lesson 3** *The Kite*

▶Staying on Topic

WRITER'S CRAFT

> **Rule** Writers write sentences that tell about one topic.

Practice Draw a line through the sentence that does not belong.

1. Lizards like warm weather. Many lizards live in deserts. ~~Flowers grow on a cactus~~. The lizards go under the sand when it is hot.

2. Many animals live on mountains. Mountain goats live on mountains. They have feet that help them climb and hold onto rocks. They have fur that keeps them warm. ~~People climb mountains for fun~~.

Staying on Topic • Reteach: Comprehension and Language Arts Skills

▶Drawing Conclusions

▶Look at the picture. Circle the word that best completes each sentence.

1. Sam is (happy, sad).

2. Sam is in the (city, country).

3. Sam lives on a (farm, ranch).

4. Sam likes (pigs, horses).

COMPREHENSION

▶ Drawing Conclusions

▶ Look at each picture. Circle the phrase that best finishes each sentence.

1. The dog is shaking because:

   a. he is happy.

   (b. he is wet.)

   c. he is laughing.

2. The girl wears a mask when:

   a. she cleans her room.

   b. she talks to her friends.

   (c. she plays baseball.)

►Classification

Rule Many words are names of things that are parts of a group.

Practice You can find these things in or around a pond.

(frogs) <u>grass</u> (fish) (ducks) <u>flowers</u> <u>weeds</u>

VOCABULARY

► Circle the words that are things that swim in a pond. Write the words below.

1. _____ frogs _____   2. _____ fish _____

3. _____ ducks _____

► Draw a line under the words that grow in or around a pond. Write the words below.

4. _____ grass _____   5. _____ flowers _____

6. _____ weeds _____

▶ Sound Spelling Review

Rule	**Example**
▶The /ō/ sound can be spelled *oa_*:	▶boat load
▶The /ē/ sound can be spelled *ee*:	▶teen sweet
▶The /ow/ sound can be spelled *ow*:	▶how cow
▶These words have short-vowel sounds:	▶stop cut mitt

Practice Circle the word that rhymes with the spelling word.

1. now   (plow)   new

2. green   great   (keen)

3. frog   bring   (log)

4. toad   (road)   land

5. sun   (fun)   sit

6. will   win   (drill)

Name _____ Date _____

 # Possessive Pronouns

> **Rule** A possessive pronoun shows ownership.
> **Example** Rob's shirt is new. **His** shirt is new.

Practice Circle the correct possessive pronoun. Write it on the line.

1. James has a train set.

_____

__His_____ trains are made of wood.   (His)   Its

2. The dog is in the kennel.

_____

__Its_____ bark is loud.   (Its)   My

3. Lori sings a song.

_____

__Her_____ voice is pretty.   His   (Her)

4. I ride a bike to school.

_____

__My_____ bike is red.   (My)   Your

GRAMMAR AND USAGE

UNIT 7 Keep Trying • **Lesson 4** *The Garden*

▶ Sentences

WRITER'S CRAFT

> **Rule** A sentence is a group of words that tell a complete thought. It has a naming part and an action part.
>
> **Example** A sentence: Snow falls in winter.
>
> Not a sentence: falls in winter

Practice Circle the complete sentences.

1. (They fill the balloon with hot air.)

   Balloon with hot air.

2. Hot air.

   (Hot air makes the balloon rise.)

3. Goes up high.

   (The balloon goes up high.)

4. (Then the balloon pops!)

   Pops!

5. (It falls back to the ground.)

   Back to the ground.

Sentences • Reteach: Comprehension and Language Arts Skills

▶ Main Idea and Details

▶ **Circle the picture that does not belong.**

1. Main Idea: Going Fishing

Details:

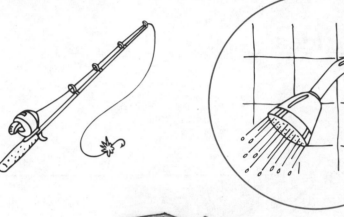

2. Main Idea: Playing Sports

Details:

▶ Main Idea and Details

▶ Match the details with the correct main idea. The first one is done for you.

COMPREHENSION

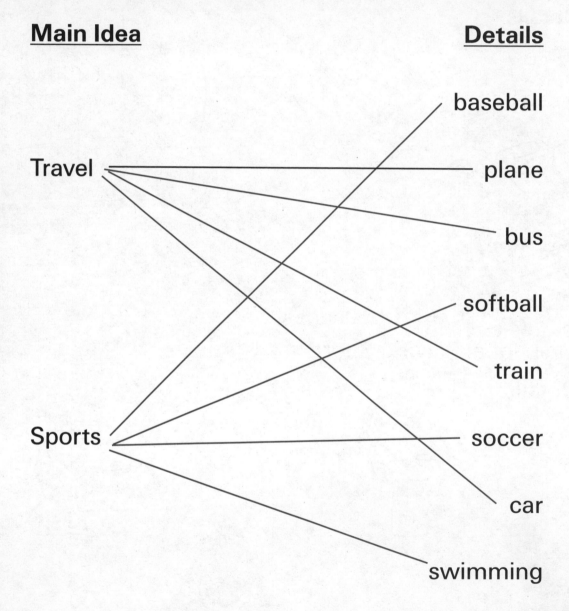

Main Idea   **Details**

baseball

Travel

plane

bus

softball

train

Sports

soccer

car

swimming

▶ Parts of a Group

> **Rule** Many words are names of things that are part of a group.

Practice Read the words below and answer the questions. One word will be used two times.

doors	rooms	horn	wheels	bricks

Which words can be parts of a house?

1. ___doors___   2. ___rooms___

3. ___bricks___

Which words can be parts of a car?

4. ___doors___   5. ___horn___

6. ___wheels___

VOCABULARY

▶ Adjectives That Compare

GRAMMAR AND USAGE

Rule

▶Add *–er* to an adjective to compare two things.

▶Add *–est* to an adjective to compare more than two things.

Practice Write the correct word on the line.

fast	faster	fastest
older	oldest	

_____ _____ _____

faster **fast** **fastest**

1. My grandpa is the _____**oldest**_____ .

2. My dad is _____**older**_____ than my brother.

▶ Sound Spelling Review

Rule	**Example**
▶The /ow/ sound can be spelled:	▶*ow* as in now
	*ou_* as in round
▶The /s/ sound can be spelled:	▶*s* as in soda
	ce as in mice
	*ci_* as in city

Practice

▶Circle the words with the /s/ sound spelled *ce*.

(piece)   barge   (face)   (raced)

▶Circle the word with the /ow/ sound spelled *ow*. Draw a line under the word with the /ow/ sound spelled *ou_*. Then, copy the words on the lines.

(down)   <u>ground</u>

- -

down, ground

SPELLING

▶Longer Sentences

WRITER'S CRAFT

> **Rule** Writers write longer sentences to tell readers more. They write words that tell how, when, or where.

Practice Look at the picture. Read the sentence. Write the word to finish the sentence.

quickly	in summer	on trails

We like to walk.

_____

Where?

  1. We like to walk _____ on trails _____.

_____

How?

  2. We like to walk _____ quickly _____.

_____

When?

  3. We like to walk _____ in summer _____.

Longer Sentences • Reteach: Comprehension and Language Arts Skills

▶Sequence

▶**Number the sentences in order. Use 1, 2, 3, 4.**

___4___ Jill and Jan ate their picnic lunch at the park.

___1___ Jill came over to Jan's house.

___3___ Jill and Jan left the house.

___2___ Jill and Jan packed a lunch.

COMPREHENSION

▶ Sequence

▶ Circle the clue words that tell when things happened.

1. Bill woke up (early) in the morning.

2. Bill brushed his teeth (before) he went downstairs.

3. (Next,) Bill greeted his dog.

4. Bill fixed some cereal (after) he let his dog outside.

5. (Then,) Bill ate his breakfast.

6. The dog barked at the door (after) breakfast.

7. (Finally,) Bill and his dog were ready for the day.

Sequence • Reteach: Comprehension
and Language Arts Skills

►Antonyms

> **Rule** Antonyms are opposites.
> **Example** big   small

Practice Draw a line from each word to its antonym.

big	slow
easy	cold
fast	sad
hot	little
happy	hard

VOCABULARY

▶Review

Circle the correct word. Write it on the line.

> **Rule** Verbs change to show that something already happened.

_____

1. Last week Uncle Joe __**came**__ to visit.

   come   (came)

> **Rule** A pronoun takes the place of a noun.
> A possessive pronoun shows ownership.

_____   _____

2. Mike ate the cake. __**He**__ ate __**it**__ .

   (He)   It   she   (it)

3. I have a brother. __**His**__ name is Josh.

   Its   (His)

> **Rule** Adjectives use –er –est to compare nouns.

_____

4. The van is __**bigger**__ than the car.

   biggest   (bigger)

Review • Reteach: Comprehension
and Language Arts Skills

Sound Spelling Review

Rule	Example
▶The /ā/ sound can be spelled:	▶*ai_* as in pain
	_ay as in tray
▶The /o͞o/ sound is spelled:	▶*oo* as in boot.
▶The /oo/ sound is spelled:	▶*oo* as in cook.
▶The /aw/ sound can be spelled:	▶*aw* as in jaw
	*au_* as in cause

SPELLING

Practice Circle the word that is spelled correctly. Write the word on the line.

1. I am learning how to ____**play**____ the piano.

   (play)   plai

2. My fingers ____**pause**____ after each note.

   pawse   (pause)

3. My ____**foot**____ can almost reach the pedals.

   fot   (foot)

► **Dialogue**

WRITER'S CRAFT

> **Rule** Writers write words that characters say. They write quotation marks at the beginning and end of the words a character says.

Practice Circle the quotation marks. Draw a line under the words that each person says.

1. "Let's help Grandpa," said Megan. "I think it would be fun."

2. "That is a good idea," said George. "We can feed the chickens."

3. "You find the grain," said Megan. "I will get the pails."

4. "I'll open this big sack," said George. "Then we can fill the pails."

5. "The chickens are clucking," said Megan. "They must be very hungry."

Dialogue • Reteach: Comprehension and Language Arts Skills

►Kinds of Sentences

Rules

- ►A telling sentence ends with a period.
- ►An asking sentence ends with a question mark.
- ►A strong feeling sentence ends with an exclamation point.

Examples

- ►My birthday is in June.

- ►When is your birthday?

- ►My birthday is in June, too!

Practice Write the end mark that goes with each kind of sentence.

1. Will you take the dog for a walk _____ **?**

2. Eddie is a good dog _____ **.**

3. Look out for that speeding car _____ **!**

4. Always look both ways before you

   cross the street _____ **. or !**

COMPREHENSION

▶Sequence

▶ **Circle the clue words that tell when things happen.**

1. Wash your hands (before) you eat.

2. Stop by my house (later.)

3. (First) feed the fish.

4. Tyler is the (next) boy in line.

5. Do your math and (then) you can play.

6. Have you seen the cat (lately)?

▶ Sequence

▶ **Put the sentences in order. Use 1, 2, and 3.**

__2__ Then he made a plan.

__1__ First Justin decided to make a kite.

__3__ Next he got the things he needed.

__3__ After his chores, the farmer had lunch.

__2__ The farmer fed the pigs when they woke up.

__1__ The rooster crowed as the sun came up.

COMPREHENSION

UNIT 8 Games • **Lesson 2** *A Game Called Piggle*

▶Synonyms

A **synonym** has a similar meaning to another word.

small   little

Practice   Read each sentence. Write the two words that can correctly complete each sentence.

hat	sofa	cup	sick
cap	couch	mug	ill

_____

1. Sam put the _____ hat or cap _____ on his head.

_____

2. I can drink from a _____ cup or mug _____ .

_____

3. Carla sat on the _____ sofa or couch _____ .

_____

4. Thomas is _____ sick or ill _____ in bed.

Synonyms • Reteach: Comprehension and Language Arts Skills

VOCABULARY

▶ Sensory Details

Rule

▶ Writers write words to tell how something looks, feels, smells, sounds, and tastes.

Practice Write the correct describing word on each line.

sandy fresh squawking salty rolling

1. _____ **squawking** _____ seagulls.

2. _____ **rolling** _____ wave.

3. _____ **sandy** _____ beach.

4. _____ **fresh** _____ air.

5. _____ **salty** _____ sea water.

WRITER'S CRAFT

COMPREHENSION

►Comparing and Contrasting

►Circle the phrase that best tells how the pictures are the same.

1.

(animals with tails)   animals with fur

2.

(animals that swim)   animals that are green

UNIT 8 Games • **Lesson 3** *Jafta*

▶ Comparing and Contrasting

▶ Circle the phrase that best tells how the pictures are the same.

1.

(people playing sports)   people throwing balls

2.

(people with short hair)   people with curly hair

3.

(wild animals)   animals with stripes

COMPREHENSION

SPELLING

▶Sound Spelling Review

The /ē/ sound can be spelled _y.   par**y**

The /aw/ sound can be spelled *aw*.   **r**aw

The /n/ sound can be spelled *kn_*.   **kn**ife

Practice

family	saw	paw	know

▶Write the word with the /ē/ sound spelled _y.

1. _____ **family** _____

▶Write the word with the /aw/ sound spelled *aw*.

2. _____ **saw or paw** _____   3. _____ **saw or paw** _____

▶Write the word with the /n/ sound spelled *kn_*.

4. _____ **know** _____

UNIT 8 Games • **Lesson 4** *Mary Mack*

▶Sentence Parts

Rule

▶Every sentence has two parts. The naming part tells who or what. The action part tells what the naming part does.

Example naming part: action part:

  The sleepy cat   rests on the pillow.

Practice Draw a line from each naming part to the correct action part to make a complete sentence.

1. The hen   swam in the bowl.

2. Sam the dog   went to the beach.

3. The fish   ate the seeds.

4. Lynn   fetches the stick.

GRAMMAR AND USAGE

Antonyms

> **Antonyms** are opposites.
>
> in   out

Practice   Circle the antonym of the underlined word.

1. The book is on the <u>bottom</u> shelf.

   (top)   low

2. Today is a <u>rainy</u> day.

   cloudy   (sunny)

3. The pillow is <u>soft</u>.

   (hard)   white

4. The boat sailed <u>under</u> the bridge.

   (over)   water

5. Tim went <u>up</u> the stairs.

   in   (down)

Antonyms • Reteach: Comprehension
and Language Arts Skills

VOCABULARY

UNIT 8 Games • **Lesson 5** *Matthew and Tilly*

▶Sound Spelling Review

The /j/ sound can be spelled:	*j*	as in	jail
	ge	as in	rage
The /r/ sound can be spelled:	*r*	as in	rose
	*wr_*	as in	wrong

Practice

age	phone	write	jump	that	rode

▶ Write the words that have the /j/ sound spelled *j* and *ge*.

1. ____age____   2. ____jump____

▶ Write the words that have the /r/ sound spelled *r* and *wr*.

3. ____write____   4. ____rode____

SPELLING

Reteach: Comprehension • *Sound Spelling Review* and Language Arts Skills

UNIT 8 • Lesson 5 **91**

VOCABULARY

▶ Homophones

> **Homophones** are words that sound alike. They are not spelled the same and do not mean the same.
>
> for   four

Practice Draw a line from each word to its homophone.

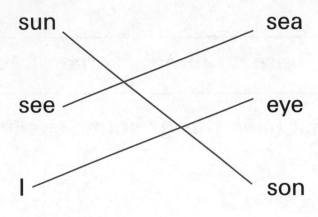

sun   sea

see   eye

I   son

hear   beat

beet   here

Homophones • Reteach: Comprehension
and Language Arts Skills

▶ Sound Spelling Review

> Short-vowel sounds can be spelled: *consonant-vowel-consonant.*
>
> pat   pen   pin   pot

Practice Circle the word that completes each sentence. Write the word on the line.

1. I _____**ran**_____ in a race.

   rain   (ran)

2. I did _____**not**_____ stop.

   (not)   note

3. You _____**can**_____ run in the next race.

   cane   (can)

4. Then it will be my turn to _____**sit**_____ and rest.

   site   (sit)

SPELLING

▶ Contractions

Rule Words can be shortened to make contractions. An apostrophe takes the place of missing letters.

Example she is   she's

Write the correct contraction on the line.

he's	we're	haven't

1. have not _____ **haven't** _____

2. we are _____ **we're** _____

3. he is _____ **he's** _____

▶ **Circle the correct contraction.**

4. <u>It is</u> time to buy new shoes.   (It's)   I'll

5. <u>We will</u> have to go tomorrow.   (We'll)   We're

Contractions • Reteach: Comprehension and Language Arts Skills

Name _____ Date _____

 # Repeating Sounds

> **Rule** Writers write words that begin with the same sound.
>
> **Example** Jelly jiggles in a jar.
>
> Balloons burst with a bang.

Write the words that begin with the same sounds.

garden	snapped	gobble	stepped

_____

1. The stick _____ **snapped** _____ when I

_____

_____ **stepped** _____ on it.

_____

2. **G**ophers _____ **gobble** _____ vegetables in

_____

the _____ **garden** _____ .

WRITER'S CRAFT

►Cause and Effect

COMPREHENSION

► **The top sentence tells what happened.**
Circle the sentence that tells why it happened.
Choose a or b.

1. The dog was very muddy.

a. It chased a rabbit in the rain.

b. It had just been given a bath.

2. Tom's leg was bleeding.

a. He saw a car go by.

b. He fell down on the sidewalk.

3. The cat sat in the tree.

a. A dog ran after the cat.

b. The cat ate some food.

4. Jessie did not pass her spelling test.

a. She watched TV and did not study.

b. She always gets good grades.

5. Dishes were piled high in the sink.

a. Mom fixed me a sandwich for lunch.

b. Mom had a big dinner party.

Cause and Effect • Reteach: Comprehension
and Language Arts Skills

UNIT 8 Games • **Lesson 7** *The Big Team Relay Race*

▶Cause and Effect

▶ Match the effect on the left with the correct cause on the right.

1. Andy fell asleep in class.

2. The grass is very tall.

3. Amy zipped up her coat.

4. The dog drank a lot of water.

5. The class is getting on the bus.

It was a cold, windy day.

It was a hot, sunny day.

Andy went to bed late.

The class is going to the zoo.

The grass was cut many weeks ago.

COMPREHENSION

▶ Synonyms and Antonyms

VOCABULARY

A **synonym** has a similar meaning to another word.

happy   glad

Practice

Draw a line from each word to its synonym.

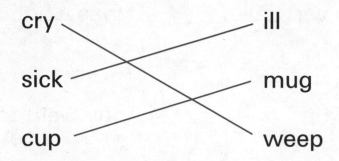

cry   ill

sick   mug

cup   weep

Antonyms are opposites.

dry   wet

Draw a line from each word to its antonym.

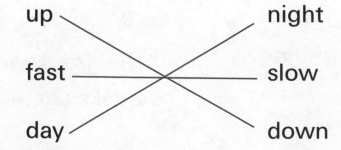

up   night

fast   slow

day   down

Review

> **Rule** There are telling sentences, asking sentences, and strong feeling sentences.

▶ **Write the end mark for each sentence.**

1. May I go on a boat ride __**?**__

2. Look at the huge whales __**!**__

> **Rule** A sentence has two parts. It has a naming part and an action part

▶ **Read the sentence. Draw a line under the naming part. Circle the action part.**

3. <u>Jordan and Eric</u> (came to my party.)

> **Rule** ' takes the place of missing letters in a contraction.

▶ **Write the contraction for the underlined words.**

4. <u>I am</u> in the first grade. __**I'm**__

▶A Paragraph That Describes

WRITER'S CRAFT

Rule	Example
▶The first sentence tells what the writer will describe. The other sentences describe it.	▶A ball is a toy. It is round. It is made of rubber. A ball is a fun, bouncing toy.

Practice **Write the sentences in a paragraph.**

It has two round sides.

A yo-yo is a toy.

A long string is in the middle.

Anyone can play with a yo-yo.

_____

A yo-yo is a toy. It has two round sides. A long string is in

_____

the middle. Anyone can play with a yo-yo.

_____

_____

▶ Sound Spelling Review

The /aw/ sound can be spelled *aw*.	cl<u>aw</u>
The /m/ sound can be spelled *mb*.	co<u>mb</u>
The /ē/ sound can be spelled *ea*.	l<u>ea</u>p

 **Read the sentences. Circle the word that is spelled correctly. Write the word on the line.**

(draw)

1. I can _____ a picture.

drau

_____

draw

(lamb)

2. Pet the wooly _____ .

lam

_____

lamb

eet

3. Please _____ your carrots.

(eat)

_____

eat

eech

4. You may _____ have a cookie.

(each)

_____

each

SPELLING

UNIT 9 Being Afraid • **Lesson I** *Unit Introduction*

▶ # Review

| **Rule** Nouns are names for people, places, and things. |
| **Example** boy   house   apple |

▶ **Read each sentence. Find and circle eight nouns.**

1. The (dog) chased the (cat) up the (tree).

2. (Alex) went to the (store).

3. The (teacher) put the (paper) on the (desk).

▶ **Write pronouns to replace the underlined words.**

| him | We | her | He |

_____   _____

We   him

1. Amy and I went to the park with Peter.

_____   _____

She   her

2. Grandma gave Lisa a hug.

GRAMMAR AND USAGE

▶ Drawing Conclusions

▶ Look at each picture. Circle the best answers.

1. How does Greg feel?

   (a. unhappy)   b. happy

2. Why does he feel this way?

   a. His book bag is big.

   (b. His book bag is torn.)

3. How does Kate feel?

   a. glad   (b. angry)

4. Why does she feel this way?

   (a. Her plane is stuck in a tree.)

   b. She likes to look at trees.

5. How does Puff the cat feel?

   (a. afraid)   b. brave

6. Why does it feel this way?

   (a. The big dog is barking at it.)

   b. Puff wants to hunt mice.

COMPREHENSION

UNIT 9 Being Afraid • **Lesson 2** *My Brother Is Afraid of Just About Everything*

▶Drawing Conclusions

▶Read the story. Put an X in front of the best answer. Then follow the directions after each question.

The sun just came up. Shana digs her toes into the sand. She looks at the deep blue water. Then Shana takes her pail and begins to pick up shells.

1. Where is Shana?

  X at the beach   __ at her school

Draw a line under the words that tell you this.

2. What time of day is it?

  X morning   __ night

Draw a circle around the sentence that tells you this.

Drawing Conclusions • Reteach: Comprehension and Language Arts Skills

▶Synonyms

> **Rule** A **synonym** has a similar meaning to another word.
> **Example** jump hop

Read each sentence. Write the word that can replace the underlined word on the line.

jog	friend	scared	hat	cold

1. My brother is <u>afraid</u> of the dark.   scared

2. I like to <u>run</u> around the block.   jog

3. My <u>cap</u> blew off in the wind.   hat

4. The <u>cool</u> water splashed my face.   cold

5. Always swim with a <u>buddy</u>.   friend

VOCABULARY

SPELLING

▶ Sound Spelling Review

Rule	**Example**
▶The /ā/ sound can be spelled:	▶_*ay* as in l<u>ay</u> *ai_* as in p<u>ai</u>n *a_e* as in t<u>a</u>k<u>e</u>
▶The /ō/ sound can be spelled *o_e* as in ph<u>o</u>n<u>e</u>.	

Practice

▶Write the spelling word that rhymes with each word below.

train	way	face	those

_____   _____

1. nose ____*those*____   2. play ____*way*____

_____   _____

3. rain ____*train*____   4. trace ____*face*____

Sound Spelling Review • Reteach: Comprehension
and Language Arts Skills

▶End Rhyme

> **Rule** Writers use rhyming words to write poems.
> **Example** Little plants in a **row**,
> Start to sprout and **grow**.

Circle the word that rhymes with the underlined word. Write the word on the line.

1. On a trip we <u>went</u>

_____

Camping in a ___tent___

cabin (tent)

2. A train chugs along a <u>track</u>,

_____

Taking people there and ___back___

(back) here

3. Up in the <u>sky</u>,

_____

I watch the plane ___fly___

(fly) glide

WRITER'S CRAFT

▶ Context Clues

VOCABULARY

> **Rule** **Context clues** are words that help you figure out what a hard word might mean.
> **Example** The <u>pilot</u> flew the plane.
> Hard Word: pilot
> Context Clues: flew, plane

Practice Read each sentence. Use the context clues to help you decide which word to write on the line.

_____

- - - - - - - - -

1. Kim _____*sits*_____ down in a chair.

   sits   swings   runs

_____

- - - - - - - - -

2. John wears a _____*belt*_____ around his waist.

   hat   shoe   belt

_____

- - - - - - - - -

3. Mary lives in a blue _____*house*_____ with seven rooms.

   pool   house   car

▶Review

Rule Verbs are action words

Example We **play** games.

Practice Read the sentences. Circle the verb in each sentence.

1. James (tosses) the ball to Karen.

2. Amy (runs) faster than Andy.

3. Charlie (jumps) up to catch the ball.

4. Sarah (yells) to her teammate.

5. Devin and Todd (race) to the bench.

6. Our team (scores) the most.

7. All of us (clap) for the winning team.

GRAMMAR AND USAGE

Name _____ Date _____

SPELLING

▶ Sound Spelling Review

Rule		**Example**	
▶ The /ē/ sound can be spelled:	*ee*	as in	<u>fee</u>t
	_*y*	as in	an<u>y</u>
▶ The /ū/ sound can be spelled *ew* as in few.			
▶ Short vowel sounds can be spelled with different patterns.			

Practice

▶ Circle the word that rhymes with the spelling word.

1. beg   bug   (leg)

2. clap   (map)   clock

3. few   (pew)   fell

4. deep   sled   (keep)

▶ Circle the words that use _*y* to make the /ē/ sound.

yes   (silly)   play

(party)   boy   (baby)

▶The Suffix -er

Rule A **suffix** is added to the end of a word. The suffix -*er* changes a word so that it means "more."

Example small + er = "more small"

The mouse is <u>smaller</u> than the cat.

Practice Draw a line from the word with -*er* added to the words that tell what it means.

<u>higher</u>	more cold
<u>taller</u>	more warm
<u>faster</u>	more high
<u>colder</u>	more tall
<u>warmer</u>	more fast

VOCABULARY

UNIT 9 Being Afraid • **Lesson 5** *Strange Bumps*

▶Review

Rule	**Example**
▶A telling sentence ends with a period.	▶I like to run.
▶An asking sentence ends with a question mark.	▶Do you like to run?
▶A strong feeling sentence ends with an exclamation point.	▶Hey, slow down!

Write the correct end mark at the end of each sentence. Draw a line under the telling sentence. Circle the asking sentence. Draw a box around the strong feeling sentence.

1. What is your name ___?___

2. My name is Beth ___.___

3. I am so happy to meet you ___!___

Review • Reteach: Comprehension and Language Arts Skills

►Comparing and Contrasting

► **Circle the word that tells what these sentences are about.**

1. Bob wants to play football when he is older.

2. Jill likes going to softball practice after school.

3. Ben's sister plays tennis every weekend.

(sports)   recess

1. Sara has four brothers and one sister.

2. Bill is going to visit his aunt and uncle.

3. Fred has fun with his grandparents.

visiting   (relatives)

COMPREHENSION

►Comparing and Contrasting

COMPREHENSION

►Circle the word that is different.

1. top   top   top   (mop)

2. pig   (peg)   pig   pig

3. mile   mile   (smile)   mile

4. (seat)   eat   eat   eat

5. quick   quick   (quack)   quick

6. mule   (mole)   mule   mule

7. dew   dew   dew   (do)

Name _____ Date _____

▶Sound Spelling Review

Rule

▶The /ū/ sound can be spelled *u, u_e, _ew,* or *_ue.*

▶The /o͞o/ sound can be spelled, *u, u_e, _ew, oo,* or *_ue.*

▶The /kw/ sound is spelled *qu_* as in queen.

Practice

| unit | quit | grew | soon | quick |

▶**Write the word that rhymes with each word below.**

1. blew _____**grew**_____   2. moon _____**soon**_____

▶**Write a word beginning with the same sound.**

3. quiet _**quit or quick**_   4. uniform _____**unit**_____

5. quilt _**quit or quick**_

SPELLING

▶Review

GRAMMAR AND USAGE

> **Rule** Adjectives tell more about nouns.
> **Example** That is a **big black** bug.

> **Rule**
> ▶ Add -er to an adjective to compare two things.
> ▶ Add -est to compare more than two things.

Draw a line under the words that describe a noun.

1. It is a <u>hot</u> <u>sunny</u> day.

2. I found a <u>smooth</u> <u>shiny</u> stone.

3. Mom made <u>cold</u> <u>sweet</u> lemonade.

Write the correct word below each picture.

bright	brighter	brightest

  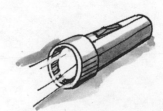

brightest   brighter   bright

Cause and Effect

▶ The top sentence tells what happened.
Read it and then circle the sentence
that best tells why it happened.

1. The dog caught the ball.
   a. Mark threw the ball to the dog.
   b. The ball fell out of the tree.

2. Jill was crying.
   a. It was her birthday.
   b. She hurt her knee.

3. Ben drank a big glass of water.
   a. He was thristy.
   b. He was sleepy.

4. Ron hit the ball with his bat.
   a. He was swimming.
   b. He was playing baseball.

COMPREHENSION

▶Cause and Effect

▶**Match each effect with the best cause.**

Effect	Cause

Effect

1. The dog was dirty.

2. Sue ate an apple.

3. Ron went home early.

4. The cat was wet when she came inside.

5. Bill was tired.

6. Jim gave his mom some flowers.

7. Sara tiptoed around the house.

8. Jill picked her baby brother up.

Cause

She was hungry.

It was raining outside.

He stayed up late last night.

He sat in the mud.

Her sister was sleeping.

He was sick.

He was crying.

It was her birthday.

Cause and Effect • Reteach: Comprehension and Language Arts Skills

Name _____ Date _____

►Compound Words

> **Rule** A compound word is a word made from two words.
>
> **Example** bee + hive = beehive

Practice Read each sentence. Circle the word that will correctly complete the compound word and write it on the line.

_____

1. Today is my birth___**day**___.

  mark   (day)

_____

2. I invited every___**one**___ to my party.

  thing   (one)

_____

3. My mom made cup___**cakes**___.

  (cakes)   board

_____

4. Max gave me a pet gold___**fish**___.

  smith   (fish)

VOCABULARY

▶ Sound Spelling Review

SPELLING

Rule	Example
▶The /ow/ sound can be spelled:	▶*ou_* as in <u>ou</u>ch *ow* as in d<u>ow</u>n.
▶The /er/ sound can be spelled *ir* as in b<u>ir</u>d.	
▶The /ō/ sound can be spelled _*ow* as in sl<u>ow</u>.	
▶The /ē/ sound can be spelled _*y* as in man<u>y</u>.	
▶The /ī/ sound can be spelled _*y* as in sl<u>y</u>.	

Practice

throw	dirt	dry	clown	story	out

▶ **Write the spelling word that rhymes with each word below.**

1. shirt _____dirt_____   **2.** frown _____clown_____

3. fry _____dry_____   **4.** blow _____throw_____

5. trout _____out_____   **6.** glory _____story_____

▶Review

GRAMMAR AND USAGE

Rule	**Example**
▶ Add **-ed** to a verb to show that it already happened.	▶ The parade **marched** through town.
▶ Some verbs change to show that something already happened. They don't use **-ed**.	▶ Chris **saw** a clown.

Practice Circle the past tense verb in each sentence.

1. Jamie and Chris (played) in the park.

2. They (watched) the insects.

3. Chris (caught) a bug.

4. Jamie (skipped) high.

5. The children (laughed).

6. Jamie (sat) down to rest.

▶Review

VOCABULARY

> **Remember** **Context clues** are words that help you figure out what a hard word might mean.
>
> **Remember** A **synonym** has almost the same meaning as another word.
>
> **Remember** A **compound word** is a word made from two words.

▶ **Read and answer the questions below.**

The angry policeman blew his whistle at the cars. They were driving faster than the speed limit allowed.

1. Circle the **context clues** for the word *whistle*.

   angry   (policeman)   (blew)

2. Circle the words that are **synonyms** for *angry*.

   (mad)   kind   (upset)

3. Circle the word that is a **compound word**.

   (policeman)   whistle   allowed

▶Rhythm

> **Rule** Rhythm is a repeated beat.
> **Example**   Pease porridge hot,
> Pease porridge cold,
> Pease porridge in the pot,
> Nine days old!

Practice Read each poem. Circle the poems that have the same rhythm.

1. Up, up, up,

   Jumps the pup!

2. Skip, run

   Have lots of fun,

   Jump, hop

   To the top!

3. Go, go, go,

   Runs the doe.

4. High, high, high

   Goes the balloon

   Fly, fly, fly

   To the moon.

WRITER'S CRAFT

UNIT 9 Being Afraid • **Lesson II** *Unit Wrap-Up*

SPELLING

►Sound Spelling Review

> **Rule**
> ► The /ng/ sound can be spelled *ng* as in ba<u>ng</u>.
> ► The /aw/ sound can be spelled *aw* as in j<u>aw</u>.
> ► Long vowel sounds can end in *r* as in f<u>air</u>.

Practice Write the spelling word that best completes each sentence.

law	sting	fling	fawn	stair	roar

_____

1. The _____ **fawn** _____ ran out from the woods.

2. We heard the lion _____ **roar** _____ at the zoo.

3. The monkey can _____ **fling** _____ the banana in the air.

4. Don't trip as you walk down the last _____ **stair** _____.

Sound Spelling Review • Reteach: Comprehension and Language Arts Skills

▶Review

> **Rule** The naming part of a sentence agrees with the verb in the action part.
>
> **Example** Pam walks home. They walk home.

Practice Circle the verb that agrees with the naming part. Write it on the line.

1. Max __catches__ the ball.

  catch (catches)

2. Emily __digs__ in the garden.

  dig (digs)

3. Mom and Luis __share__ a pie.

  (share) shares

4. They __wash__ the dishes.

  (wash) washes

COMPREHENSION

▶ Classifying and Categorizing

▶Read each set of words. Find the category in the box that matches each set of words. Then write the category below the set of words.

| parts of a person's body | parts of an animal's body |

Set 1

      skin   fingernails

      hand   foot

_____

parts of a person's body

Set 2

      paw   tail

      fur   claw

_____

parts of an animal's body

▶Classifying and Categorizing

▶**Find the word in the box that goes with each word.**

cub	puppy	tadpole
calf	lamb	

1. dog   and

2. frog   and

3. bear   and

4. cow   and

5. sheep   and

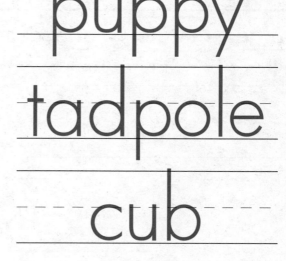

puppy

tadpole

cub

calf

lamb

COMPREHENSION

▶ Parts of a Group

VOCABULARY

> **Rule** Many words name things that are part of a group.

Practice

▶Draw a line under the words that name numbers.
Write the words on the lines below.

nine	circle	one	square	triangle	four

1. _____nine_____

2. _____one_____

Order of answers may vary.

3. _____four_____

▶ Circle the words that name shapes.
Write the words on the lines below.

1. _____circle_____

2. _____square_____

3. _____triangle_____

Parts of a Group • Reteach: Comprehension
and Language Arts Skills

▶Sound Spelling Review

SPELLING

Rules

▶The /ch/ sound can be spelled *ch* as in <u>ch</u>air.

▶The /oi/ sound can be spelled *_oy* as in j<u>oy</u>.

▶The /j/ sound can be spelled ▪*dge* as in fu<u>dge</u>.

▶The /s/ sound can be spelled *ce* as in ni<u>ce</u>.

Practice Write the spelling word that best completes each sentence.

enjoying   cement

_____

1. The _____ **cement** _____ on the driveway is hot.

2. We are _____ **enjoying** _____ this sunny afternoon.

▶Circle the correct spelling for each word. Write the spelling word on the line.

3. juge   (judge)   juj   _____ **judge** _____

4.(chimney)   shimney   schimney   _____ **chimney** _____

COMPREHENSION

▶ Classifying and Categorizing

▶ Put an **X** next to each sentence that tells about homes.

X Rabbits' homes are underground in burrows.

X The birds built their home in our apple tree.

____ Sara could not go out to play because it was raining.

X Our house sits on a big hill.

▶ Classifying and Categorizing

▶ Read each set of words. Find the category in the box that matches each set of words. Then write the category below the set of words.

things that are wet	things that are dry

Set 1

dirt   desert

sand   dust

_____

things that are dry

Set 2

ocean   river

pond   pool

_____

things that are wet

►Parts of a Group

VOCABULARY

> **Rule** Many words name things that are part of a group.

Practice Draw a line from each word to the words that belong in that group.

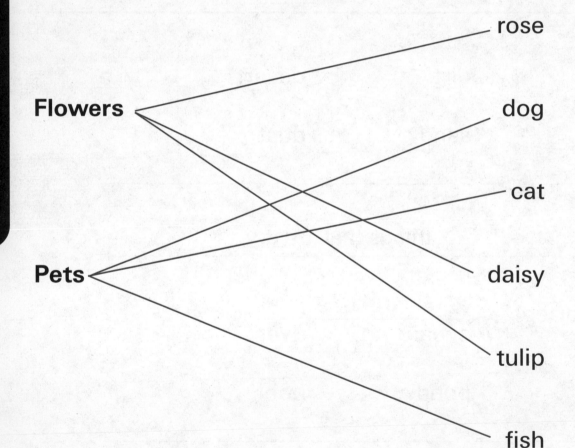

Flowers

Pets

rose

dog

cat

daisy

tulip

fish

Parts of a Group • Reteach: Comprehension and Language Arts Skills

UNIT 10 Homes • **Lesson 4** *A House Is a House for Me*

▶ Sound Spelling Review

> **Rule** The /ar/ sound is spelled *ar*.

Practice Write the spelling word that rhymes with each word.

garden	barn	started	sharp

1. yarn _____ **barn** _____

2. harden _____ **garden** _____

3. charted _____ **started** _____

4. harp _____ **sharp** _____

▶ Review

GRAMMAR AND USAGE

> **Rule** Words can be shortened to make contractions. An apostrophe takes the place of missing letters.
>
> **Example**   can not   can't
>
> The apostrophe takes the place of the **o** in **not**.

Practice Read each sentence. Write the contraction for the underlined words.

1. <u>Let us</u> play ball. _____**Let's**_____

2. <u>I will</u> join you! _____**I'll**_____

3. <u>She is</u> on my team. _____**She's**_____

4. <u>Do not</u> drop the ball! _____**Don't**_____

▶ Exact Words

Rule Writers write exact naming words, action words, and words that describe.

Examples

▶ People enjoy nibbling sweet, ripe strawberries.

▶ The bright red berry hangs from a long thin stem.

Practice Read each sentence. Circle the word that tells more. Write it on the line.

1. A _____ **blackberry** _____ grows on a vine.

   berry ⬭blackberry⬭

2. The stems have _____ **prickly** _____ thorns.

   ⬭prickly⬭ some

3. Blackberries turn dark _____ **purple** _____.

   color ⬭purple⬭

WRITER'S CRAFT

▶Compound Words

VOCABULARY

> **Rule**
> A **compound word** is a word made from two words.
>
> rain + coat = raincoat
>
> **Example**
> A <u>coat</u> to wear in the <u>rain</u> is called a **raincoat**.

Practice Read each sentence. Circle the word that will correctly complete the compound word and write it on the line.

_____

1. It is raining out _____**side**_____ .

field (side)

2. I felt a rain _____**drop**_____ on my cheek.

(drop) bow

3. Does any _____**one**_____ have an umbrella?

(one) thing

Compound Words • Reteach: Comprehension and Language Arts Skills

▶**Review**

> **Rule** Add **'s** to a noun to show that it is a possessive noun.
> **Example** ▶Bill's shoes

> **Rule** A possessive pronoun takes the place of a possessive noun.
> **Example** Bill's shoes are blue. **His** shoes are blue.

Practice Read each sentence. Circle the possessive noun or pronoun.

1. The (clown's) shoes are big.

2. (Roger's) ice cream cone tastes good.

3. (Marsha's) shorts have stripes.

4. Marsha dropped (her) ice cream cone.

5. The clown gave Roger (his) balloon.

6. (My) friends like going to the fair.

GRAMMAR AND USAGE

▶ Main Idea and Details

COMPREHENSION

▶ **Place an X next to the details that belong with each main idea.**

1. Main Idea: Tools for
Cooking Breakfast

Details:

___ top

_X_ frying pan

_X_ toaster

_X_ fork

___ car

2. Main Idea: Music

Details:

_X_ song

_X_ band

___ cow

___ apple

_X_ drum

3. Main Idea: Weather

Details:

_X_ snow

___ banana

_X_ rain

___ fence

_X_ sunshine

4. Main Idea: Beach

Details:

___ clock

_X_ sand

___ lamp

_X_ water

_X_ seashell

Main Idea and Details • Reteach: Comprehension
and Language Arts Skills

▶ Main Idea and Details

▶ **Circle the details that do not belong with the main idea.**

Main Idea: School

Details:

teacher	desk	(car)
playground	math	reading
student	drawing	recess
(bedtime)	pencil	books
homework	(dinner)	writing

COMPREHENSION

UNIT 10 Homes • **Lesson 6** *Make a Home*

▶ Sound Spelling Review

SPELLING

Rule	**Example**
▶The /f/ sound can be spelled *f* or *ph*	▶<u>f</u>un <u>ph</u>one
▶The /k/ sound can be spelled *c, k,* or ▮*ck*. The ▮*ck* is never at the beginning of a word	▶<u>c</u>at <u>k</u>it ba<u>ck</u>
▶The /a/ sound can be followed by *r*	▶c<u>ar</u>ry

Practice Write the spelling word that best completes each sentence.

carrying	skunks	finds

_____

1. The bear _____finds_____ fish in the stream.

2. I am _____carrying_____ my backpack.

3. The _____skunks_____ have black fur with white markings.

Sound Spelling Review • **Reteach: Comprehension and Language Arts Skills**

UNIT 10 Homes • **Lesson 6** *Make a Home*

▶ Sensory Details

> **Rule** Writers write words that tell how something looks, feels, smells, tastes, and sounds.

Practice Write the correct describing word on each line.

cold	fresh	chattering	fuzzy

1. Denise put on _____ fuzzy _____ slippers.

2. The _____ cold _____ lemonade tasted good.

3. The _____ chattering _____ monkey wanted a banana.

4. The flowers smelled _____ fresh _____.

WRITER'S CRAFT

▶Making Inferences

▶Look at the picture. Mark an X next to each sentence that best tells what is happening.

___ It is winter.

_X_ The children are skating in the park.

_X_ People can rest on park benches.

___ The children had sandwiches for lunch.

Making Inferences • Reteach: Comprehension and Language Arts Skills

▶ Making Inferences

▶ Read each sentence and question. For each question, circle two answers that make sense.

1. Mom packed a big basket of food for the family. Why?

   a. They were going to the park for a picnic.

   b. They were going to take a long car trip.

   c. They were going to the living room.

2. She went to sleep earlier than usual. Why?

   a. She wanted to see a movie late at night.

   b. She had to get up early the next morning.

   c. She was tired from playing outside all afternoon.

3. The dog looked out the window and barked. Why?

   a. The dog saw a squirrel outside.

   b. The dog was tired.

   c. The dog wanted to go outside.

COMPREHENSION

▶ Parts of a Group

VOCABULARY

> **Rule** Many words name things that are part of a group.

Practice Write each word from the box where it belongs. The first one is done for you.

carrots	pencil	thread	jam

1. peas and **carrots**

2. toast and **jam**

3. paper and **pencil**

4. needle and **thread**

Parts of a Group • Reteach: Comprehension and Language Arts Skills

Name _____ Date _____

▶Review

> **Rule** Quotation marks go around a speaker's exact words.
>
> **Example** "I like puppies," said Anna.

Practice

▶ **Read each sentence. Underline the exact words someone says. Circle the name of the speaker.**

1. "Look at the pups," said (Molly.)

2. "Which one is your favorite?" asked (Anna.)

3. "I like the gold one," answered (Molly.)

▶ **Read the sentences. Write quotation marks at the beginning and end of the exact words someone says.**

4. "I like the gold one, too," said Anna.

5. "It is so playful!" exclaimed Molly.

6. "Let's take him home," said Anna.

MECHANICS

► Sound Spelling Review

SPELLING

Rule

► The /ng/ sound can be spelled ▪ng as in ba<u>ng</u>.

► The /ing/ sound is spelled *ing* as in think<u>ing</u>.

Practice

► Write each spelling word under the
word with the same ending sound.

along	spring	growing	sang	peering

ga<u>ng</u>   bri<u>ng</u>
_____   _____

along   spring
_____   _____

sang   growing
_____   _____

                                    peering
                                    _____

▶A Friendly Letter

Rule A friendly letter has the **date**, a **greeting**, a **message**, a **closing**, and **your name**.

Practice Write the names of the parts of the letter where they belong.

_____

March 11, 2005 ──────
Date

──────
Greeting Dear Shana,

Our class went to a sea life park. We watched dolphins leap into the air. I didn't know they could leap so high!

──────────────

Message

 ────── Your friend,
Closing ──────

Jeff ──────
Your Name

WRITER'S CRAFT

▶ Reality and Fantasy

▶ **Circle Reality if the sentence refers to something that could really happen. Circle Fantasy if the sentence refers to something that is make-believe.**

1. The goose got some cake for the party.   Reality   (Fantasy)

2. John and Sam made a toy plane.   (Reality)   Fantasy

3. The children put on a play for the school.   (Reality)   Fantasy

4. George the Giraffe sang a song to the other animals.   Reality   (Fantasy)

5. The ants had a dance on Friday.   Reality   (Fantasy)

UNIT 10 Homes • **Lesson 9** *The Three Little Pigs*

▶Reality and Fantasy

▶ **Read each sentence. Write R in the box if it could really happen. Write F if it is make-believe.**

1. The cat sat in the sun and cleaned its fur.   **R**

2. The fox and the raccoon watched TV.   **F**

3. Carol's mom made some tea.   **R**

4. Dan made his bed this morning.   **R**

5. Everything in the city is yellow.   **F**

6. The crowd looked up at the plane.   **R**

COMPREHENSION

UNIT 10 Homes • **Lesson 9** *The Three Little Pigs*

▶Review

> **Rule** Many words name things that are part of a group.

Practice

▶Write the words that name things with wheels.

grass wagon flower tree bike

Order of answers may vary.

1. _____wagon_____   2. _____bike_____

▶Write the words that name things that grow.

Order of answers may vary.

3. _____tree_____   4. _____flower_____

5. _____grass_____

Review • Reteach: Comprehension and Language Arts Skills

VOCABULARY

▶Review

Rule Capital letters begin: **Example**

▶the first word of a sentence ▶**My** mom is going to have a baby.

▶special nouns ▶**C**ody, **A**ustin, and **R**iley

▶the word **I** ▶Mom says **I** will be a big help with the baby.

▶days of the week ▶**S**aturday

▶months of the year. ▶**J**anuary

MECHANICS

Practice Read each sentence. Circle the words that should begin with a capital letter.

1. (my) brother was born in (june.)

2. (he) was born at (mercy) (hospital.)

3. (on) (friday) he came home to our house on (cedar) (lane.)

4. (my) cousin (rose) came all the way from (idaho.)

5. (mom) thinks (i) am a great big sister.

UNIT 10 Homes • **Lesson 9** *The Three Little Pigs*

► Audience and Purpose

WRITER'S CRAFT

> **Rule** Writers think about who will read their writing. Then they think about what they want to tell them.
> **Example** A farmer writes a sign to sell fruit at a market.

Practice

► **Read each sentence. Circle the audience.**

1. (My teacher) read my report.

2. I sent a card to (my friend.)

3. Janet wrote a list for (Tom.)

► **Read each sentence. Underline the purpose for writing.**

1. I wrote in my journal to <u>tell about my day.</u>

2. Tomàs wrote a note to <u>thank his aunt.</u>

3. Emily wrote a story to <u>describe a funny creature.</u>

Audience and Purpose • Reteach: Comprehension and Language Arts Skills

▶ Sound Spelling Review

Rules

▶ The /oi/ sound can be spelled:

oi	as in	b<u>oi</u>l
_oy	as in	t<u>oy</u>

▶ The /er/ sound can be spelled *er, ir,* or *ur.*

Practice

▶ Write the spelling word with the same sound as the underlined part of the words below.

c<u>oi</u>n	f<u>i</u>rst

1. s<u>oi</u>l   b<u>oy</u>   p<u>oi</u>nt   _____ **coin** _____

2. b<u>ur</u>st   h<u>er</u>d   w<u>or</u>st   _____ **first** _____

SPELLING